AF471164

The description and history of the Regalia have been compiled mainly from two articles in the *Proceedings of the Society of Antiquaries of Scotland* (1889-90), namely, 'The Scottish Regalia' by J. J. Reid and 'Technical Description of the Regalia of Scotland' by A. S. Brook and from various documents in the office of the King's and Lord Treasurer's Remembrancer. Many of the illustrations have been reproduced by kind permission of the Society of Antiquaries.

Sir James Fergusson, Bt, Keeper of the Records of Scotland, has kindly read over the whole manuscript and made many valuable suggestions and corrections.

July 1951   W. D. C.

The opportunity has been taken to incorporate in the present text several alterations and amendments which have come to light since 1951. These arise mainly from suggestions by Sir James Fergusson, Bt, to whom thanks are again due.

October 1969   J. B. I. McTavish
Queen's and Lord Treasurer's Remembrancer

The Honours of Scotland

The Crown, the Sceptre and the Sword of State, the emblems of kingly power when Scotland was a separate kingdom

Information for visitors: admission to the Crown Room

HOURS OF OPENING

Summer	_Weekdays_	_Sundays_
(June*–September)	9.30 a.m.–6 p.m.	11 a.m.–6 p.m.

*_or Whitsun when earlier_

Hours slightly shortened at other times of year. For further information telephone 031-229 2585 (weekends 031-229 7242)

ADMISSION FEES

(to all Historical Apartments, including Crown Room)

Adults: 3s [15p] Summer; 2s [10p] Winter

Children: (under 15) and Old Age Pensioners*: 1s [5p]†

*_on production of pension book_   †_at all times_

Permission may be granted in advance by the Ministry of Public Building and Works to local authorities for parties of school chidren, accompanied by teachers, to see over the Historical Apartments, without charge, except during the months of June and July.

Cars and buses may be parked on the Castle Esplanade when space is available. There is a tea room open from April to September, and a room for the sale of official publications and postcards There is also a kiosk at the entrance to the Castle.

The Scottish Regalia

anciently styled 'The Honours of Scotland'

Compiled by W. D. Collier
King's and Lord Treasurer's Remembrancer

1970

Edinburgh
Her Majesty's Stationery Office

First published 1951
Second edition 1970

Printed in Scotland for Her Majesty's Stationery Office
by Robert MacLehose and Co. Ltd, the University Press, Glasgow W3

Design by HMSO: David G. Napthine

SBN 11 490332 8

From the very earliest ages there have come down to us proofs of the use of royal emblems, and in Western Europe these seem to have invariably embraced not only the Crown, but also the Sceptre and the Sword of State. The Crown serves as the distinctive personal symbol of the King; the Sceptre is the emblem of his royal power; and lastly, the Sword signifies at once justice and the right of peace and war.

The Regalia proper, the 'Honours of Scotland', consist of these symbols of royalty, and associated with them are a rod known as the Lord High Treasurer's Mace and certain jewels bequeathed to George III by Henry, Cardinal of York.

THE CROWN

The Crown which today rests in the Crown Room of Edinburgh Castle was remodelled by order of James V in 1540, but there is no precise evidence of its antiquity. Sir Walter Scott considered that the alteration of 1540 was merely the addition of the arches and not an actual replacement of the substance of the Crown which he ascribes to the reign of Robert the Bruce. There is evidence that, at least in part, it possesses a greater antiquity than 1540, for there is preserved in the National Library of Scotland a manuscript diary of Lord Fountainhall stating that 'the Crown of Scotland is not the ancient Crown but was casten of new by James V.'

In the accounts of the Lord High Treasurer of Scotland there are recorded payments in 1532 and 1533 for gold to mend the Crown, and on the 15th January 1540, to John Mosman, a goldsmith in Edinburgh, for the making and fashion of the King's Crown and for twenty-three stones supplied for it; to John Paterson, for a case to the Crown; and to Thomas Arthur, for velvet and satin and for making a

ABOVE
The bonnet of the Crown

OPPOSITE, ABOVE
The Crown without the bonnet

OPPOSITE, LEFT
The mound and cross pattée (back view)

OPPOSITE, RIGHT
The mound and cross pattée (front view)

bonnet to the Crown. The reading of these accounts together suggests a remaking of the ancient Crown and an increase in its size and weight, which is now 56 oz 5 dwt.troy.

It consists, in its lower portion, of a circle or band of gold about an inch and a half wide and nearly eight inches in diameter. On this band are 22 large stones consisting of 9 carbuncles, 4 jacinths, 4 amethysts, 3 topazes and 2 rock crystals. These stones have all been cut and polished by a lapidary and are set in gold. Between each of these settings are interposed twenty pearls, thirteen of which are believed to be of Oriental and seven of Scottish origin. The circle or band is heightened by ten crosses fleury enriched with pearls and white topazes alternating with ten fleurs-de-lis made entirely of gold and unadorned with any gems. In the triangular spaces formed by the elevation of the crosses fleury and the fleurs-de-lis there have been fixed settings of various forms—circular, square, triangular and lozenge-shaped. These settings, which are placed directly below each cross fleury and each fleur-de-lis, have been filled alternately with diamonds and blue enamel.

The four golden arches of the Crown are ornamented with gold and red enamelled oak leaves, apparently of French workmanship, and at the point where the arches meet there rests a mound or celestial globe of gold, the sign of sovereign authority and majesty, which is enamelled in blue and ornamented with gilt stars. This again is surmounted by a large cross decorated in gold and black enamel with an amethyst in rectangular form in the centre. The upper and two side extremities of the cross are adorned with fine Oriental pearls.

It is generally accepted that the gold of which the Crown is composed was obtained partly, if not entirely, from Scottish mines—probably from those of Crawford Moor, which were active about the period when the Crown was remade.

The bonnet of the Crown is of crimson silk velvet. It is not the ancient bonnet, having been renewed several times since

1818. It is adorned on each of the four quarters with a large Oriental pearl set on an oblong pierced gold ornament delicately enamelled in red, blue, green and white. Sewn to the bonnet is a band of ermine. The Crown rests on a crimson silk velvet cushion of recent manufacture.

See diagram and key to details of the Crown on pages 10/11

The symbols of sovereignty

These are the symbols of sovereignty which were associated with the Scottish Crown when Scotland was a separate kingdom:

1 The Crown (with the ancient velvet cushion)
2 The Sceptre
3 The Sword of State
4 The sword belt of the Sword of State
5 The Lord High Treasurer's mace
6 The collar and George of the Order of the Garter
7 The St Andrew of the Order of the Thistle
8 The ruby and diamond ring

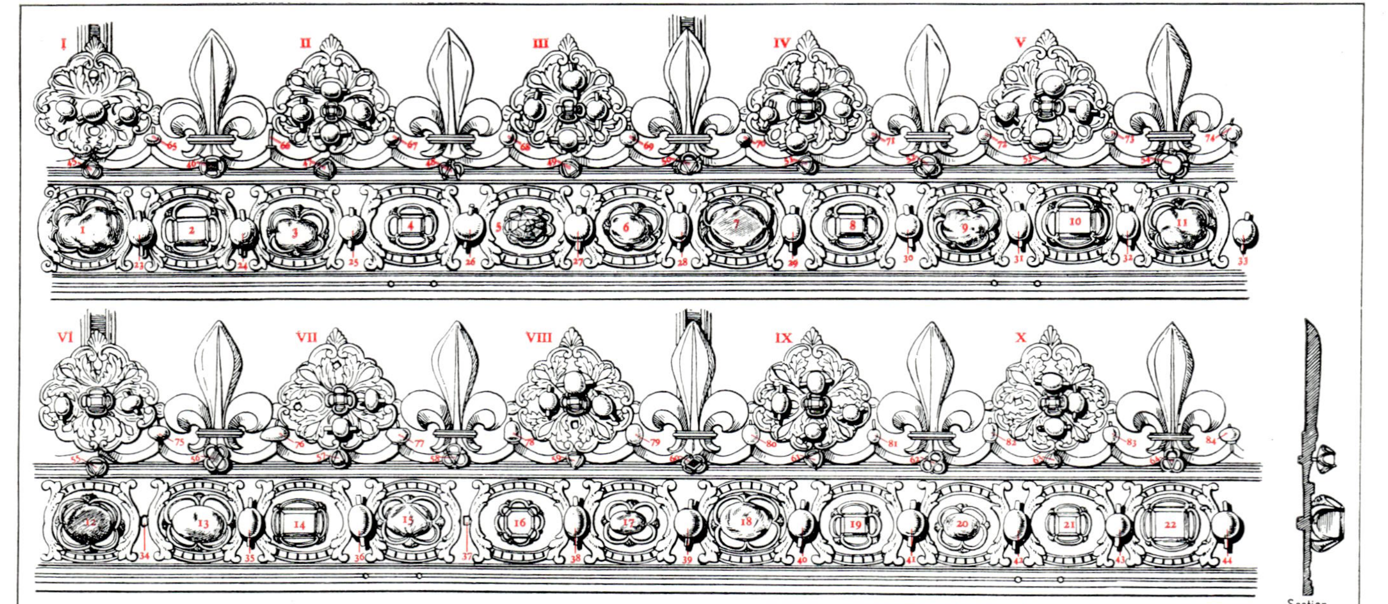

The stones and pearls on the fillet, rays and crosses of the Crown of Scotland (diagram and key)

The diagram shows the jewels on the Crown in 1707 or earlier: in 1937, some pearls etc. were added to replace those missing

STONES ON THE CIRCLE OR FILLET

1   Carbuncle, irregularly notched on the surface
2   Jacinth, rectangular in form
3   Carbuncle, irregular oval
4   Rock crystal, cut with a table (slightly domed)
5   Amethyst, cut somewhat resembling a rose diamond
6   Carbuncle, irregular in form
13   Carbuncle, irregular in form, with an unequal polished smooth surface
14   Amethyst, rectangular in form
15   Carbuncle, irregularly notched on the surface
16   Amethyst, cushion-shaped, cut with a bevelled edge
17   Carbuncle, oval in form, irregularly notched on the surface

7   White topaz, irregular polished surface (the remains of a pale green foil are visible and it may originally have been intended to represent an emerald)
8   Jacinth, rectangular in form
9   Carbuncle, irregularly notched on the surface
10 Jacinth, rectangular in form
11 Carbuncle, irregularly notched on the surface
12 White topaz, irregularly notched on the surface and polished smooth, with traces of dark green foil behind

18 White topaz, irregularly notched on the surface and polished smooth, with traces of yellow foil behind
19 Amethyst, rectangular in form
20 Carbuncle, oval in form
21 Rock crystal, cut with a table, with green foil behind
22 Jacinth, rectangular in form, cut with a table (slightly domed)

PEARLS ON THE CIRCLE OR FILLET

23, 24, 26, 28, 30, 31, 32, 38, 39, 41, 42, 43 and 44 are Oriental pearls

25, 27, 29, 33, 35, 36, and 40 are Scottish pearls. 34 and 37 both pearl and setting amissing

STONES, ETC. BELOW THE CROSSES AND FLEURS-DE-LIS

45, 47, 49, 51, 55, 57, 59, 61 and 63, triangular setting, fitted with blue enamel. 48, 50, 52, 58, 62 and 64, triangular setting, containing a diamond, table cut, with three straight bevelled edges
54 round setting containing a diamond

56 lozenge-shaped setting, containing a diamond
46 square setting, empty
60 lozenge-shaped setting, empty
53 setting amissing

PEARLS AND STONES ON THE CROSSES FLEURY

I   3 Oriental pearls
II   4 Oriental pearls, 1 white topaz in the centre
III   4 Oriental pearls, 1 white topaz in the centre
IV   4 Oriental pearls, 1 white topaz in the centre
V   4 Oriental pearls, 1 white topaz in the centre
VI   2 Oriental pearls, 1 white topaz in the centre
VII   2 Oriental pearls, 1 white topaz in the centre

VIII 3 pearls (that on the dexter arm of the cross is Oriental, the other two Scottish)
IX   4 Oriental pearls, 1 white topaz in the centre
X   3 pearls (that on the lower portion of the cross below the white topaz is Scottish, the other two are Oriental, 1 white topaz in the centre)

PEARLS ON THE POINTS OF THE RAYS

65–84 all except number 81, which is Scottish, are Oriental (number 66 is amissing, the wire standing)

THE SCEPTRE

The Sceptre was originally a gift from Rome, having been presented along with a gold rose by Pope Alexander VI to James IV in 1494. It was refashioned by James V, whose initials are engraved on the upper portion of the lower division of the rod. The design may be divided into three distinct parts—first the rod, including the handle; second the head or capital; and third, a globe of rock crystal with finial, surmounted by a Scottish pearl.

The rod, which is of gilded silver, is of hexagonal form and is in three divisions, the end division forming the handle. The second division of the rod is ornamented on three of

*Statuette of St James
on the head of the Sceptre
(actual size)*

*Statuette of St Andrew
on the head of the Sceptre
(actual size)*

ABOVE *Head of the Sceptre (actual size)*

RIGHT *Head of the Sceptre, with the globe of rock crystal and finial*

Engraved ornamentation on the rod of the Sceptre (scale $\frac{3}{5}$)

its six sides with engraved fleurs-de-lis and thistles, while the upper division is decorated on three of its sides with grotesques, cups, and foliage.

The head of the rod is flanked by dolphins, between which are placed three small figures. The first of these represents the Virgin Mary, crowned with an open crown, holding on her right arm Our Saviour and in her left hand a mound, ensigned with a cross. On her left hand is St James, clad in a loose flowing robe and cape with the collar fastened at the neck. His right hand is raised and holds an open book. In his left hand is a staff, the head of which is broken off. To his left is St Andrew in an apostolical robe with cape, holding in his right hand a St Andrew's cross or saltire, the upper portion of which is broken off, and in his left hand, elevated, an open book.

Above this group is a globe of rock crystal, cut and polished smooth, and this again is surmounted by a small oval globe on the top of which is fixed a Scottish pearl.

THE SWORD OF STATE

The Sword of State was presented by Pope Julius II to James IV in 1507. It was accompanied by the sword belt and a consecrated hat, and they were delivered with great solemnity in the Church of Holyrood by the Papal legate and the Abbot of Dunfermline. It is a fine specimen of craftsmanship and belongs to the period when the art of sculpture was reviving in Rome.

OPPOSITE
*The handle
and guard
of the Sword
of State*

*Arms of
Pope Julius II,
enamelled on
the scabbard
of the
Sword of State
(actual size)*

The blade of the Sword is 3 feet 3 inches long and carries two gold-filled etchings of the apostles Paul and Peter, once concealed by ornamental leaves which are now broken away. In the centre of the blade on each side there is also etched and filled in with gold the name of Pope Julius. Oak leaves and acorns, the emblem of Pope Julius, are heavily sculptured on the pommel and handle, which are made of gilded silver. The traverse guard of the Sword is $17\frac{1}{4}$ inches from extremity to extremity and in design consists of two

Etching of the Apostle Paul
on the blade of the Sword of State
(*actual size*)

Etching of the Apostle Peter
on the blade of the Sword of State
(*actual size*)

dolphins looking towards the handle, with their tails terminating in an acorn and oak leaves, which form the ends of the cross.

The scabbard is made of wood, covered with crimson silk velvet and mounted with silver-gilt ornamentation and enamelled plates; one of these bears the arms of Pope Julius II, and two of the others bear some letters which evidently formed part of the Pope's cipher.

Etching of the name of Pope Julius II on the blade of the Sword of State (actual size)

A Brief History of the Regalia

One of the very earliest instances of royal inauguration by the hands of an ecclesiastic is found in Scotland, where Saint Columba, the apostle of national Christianity, officiated at the accession of King Aidan at Iona, in 574 AD. But though the early kings of the Scots are depicted on their seals and elsewhere as wearing crowns, there is no record of coronation being a part of the ceremony of their inauguration. They were consecrated and 'set in the royal seat' at Scone. Malcolm IV was thus inaugurated on 24th May 1153, in presence of a great assembly, Alexander II in 1214 and Alexander III in 1249. At the ceremony marking the accession of Alexander II it is recorded that the 'seven Earls of Scotland' were present in their order—Fife, Stratherne, Athol, Angus, Menteith, Buchan and Lothian. The manner in which they are referred to leads to the conclusion that their presence was official, and formed an important item in the ceremonial. Subsequent events in history suggest that the ancient Earls of Fife enjoyed the special privilege of placing the crown upon the King's head, and it is probable that other duties would be assigned to each of the other Earls. It is clear therefore that as early as the beginning of the thirteenth century recognised ceremonies marked the accession of a Scottish king, though not till a century later did they include coronation and anointing.

After the reign of Alexander III it must be concluded that the Honours of Scotland in their proper sense—that is to say, the Crown, the Sceptre and the Sword, certainly existed, for we are told that Alexander's luckless successor, John Baliol, was deprived of these royal emblems by Edward I at Montrose in 1296. So the Regalia of those early days went across the Border never to return and probably vanished later under the Commonwealth. When Robert the Bruce raised the standard of Scottish independence, there was thus no Crown existing and in 1306 a golden circlet was hastily made and was placed upon his head by a lady of the Macduff family in whom, as already shown, the hereditary right seems to have been vested. Even this hastily contrived Crown was carried off to England as part of the plunder after Bruce's disaster at Methven later in the same year. None of the records supply evidence, after Scotland secured her freedom on the field of Bannockburn, that the Honours of the Kingdom were replaced until we come to the accession of David II in 1331, when the

Exchequer Rolls record a payment to Copyn, the goldsmith, for making a small Sceptre for the boy king. The coronation took place at Scone, but from the time of David II until that of James IV there is nothing to record concerning the three main articles which composed the Regalia. All we can safely assume is that they must have been in existence and were used at each successive coronation. All these coronations took place at Scone, excepting those of James II at Holyrood in 1437 and James III when but nine years old at Kelso Abbey in 1460.

When we come to the reign of James IV, he is described by an Act of Parliament as sitting in 1503 *'regalibus trabeatus et vestitus coronam capite sceptrum regium manu gestans'*, and the Lord Treasurer's accounts of the year before show a payment to a Robert Selkirk, cutler, for the great Sword of Honour and for making a sheath to the same. Five years later, the new Sword of State now exhibited was presented by Pope Julius II; and King James V, who was fond of altering and adding to the weight and value of the royal emblems, instructed, as indicated above, that the Sceptre should be melted down and remodelled and that the Crown be refashioned. So we come to the time when the Honours can be directly connected with those now in the Crown Room at Edinburgh Castle.

There is nothing to record of the Regalia at the coronation of Queen Mary or during her early days. She was crowned at Stirling in 1543 when but nine months old. At the close of her unfortunate reign, however, we are once more brought into touch with the Honours. When Mary, in 1568, crossed the Border never to return, her adherents, still numerous and powerful, retained possession of Edinburgh Castle under the command of Sir William Kirkcaldy of Grange. In this stronghold the Honours were kept for greater security, and when in 1571 the young King's party wished to hold a Parliament in Stirling, some substitute had to be found. The Lord Treasurer's accounts indicate that a silvergilt Crown and Sceptre and a Sword of State were hastily improvised, no doubt 'becaus the principall jewellis wer in the Castell of Edinburgh, and mycht not be haid'. In April 1573 an attempt was made unsuccessfully to induce the Governor of the Castle to give up the Regalia, but in the following month starvation forced Kirkcaldy to surrender and the Honours fell into the hands of the King's adherents.

By an Act of Parliament passed in 1585, the custody of the Honours was included in the commission of the Captain of Edinburgh Castle and there is nothing of importance to relate concerning them beyond their production when Parliament was

sitting until we come to the coronation of Charles I at Holyrood
on 18th June 1633.

Charles the First

We are told that the coronation procession was on horseback and
proceeded from the Castle to Holyrood. First came the Barons,
Bishops, Viscounts and Earls, two by two in the order named and
preceded by six trumpeters in scarlet and gold. Next followed
the Archbishop of Glasgow, the Lord Privy Seal, the Lord
Treasurer and Lord Chancellor, various heraldic dignitaries, the
Lord High Almoner and the Lord Lyon King of Arms. Then
followed the Regalia, the Crown borne by the Marquis of
Douglas, supported on his right by the Great Constable, and on
his left by the Great Chamberlain and the Earl Marischall, the
Sceptre being borne by the Earl of Rothes and the Sword of
State by the Earl of Buchan. Immediately after the Crown came
the King himself. On arrival at Holyrood, dismounting under a
crimson velvet canopy, Charles was met by the Archbishop of
St Andrews and the other prelates who were to take part in the
religious ritual. After the religious ceremony the coronation
proper began. The Archbishop pronounced a short prayer and
then placed the Crown upon Charles's head. The King wore the
royal robe of King James IV, the last monarch to have been
crowned as an adult, nearly 150 years before. The Sword of
State was ungirt by the Great Chamberlain and placed upon the
communion table by the Archbishop, who then placed the
Sceptre in the King's right hand. The proceedings ended with a
return procession on foot, Charles wearing the royal robe and
Crown and carrying the Sceptre, while salvos of artillery rang
out from the Castle.

At the beginning of the Scottish Civil Wars in 1637, the
Regalia appear to have been removed, apparently as a security
measure, from Edinburgh Castle to Dalkeith. Some two years
later, however, the King's house at Dalkeith as well as the Castle
fell into the hands of the Covenanters who took the 'royall
ornamentis of the Crown, sic as croun, suord, and scepter, and
had thame to the Castell of Edinburgh.' The Honours were used
at the assembling of Parliament a few months later, when they
were borne before the Earl of Traquair, the Commissioner. A
narrator of these events was profoundly shocked at what followed
when Parliament reassembled after adjournment on 11th June

1640, for he relates, 'Whilk day being cum the parliament sat doune wanting ane King or Commissioner, quhairof the like was never seen in the Christean worlde.'

After the defeat of Charles I at Newburn in August 1640, the Honours remained in the possession of the Presbyterian party during those eventful years which embraced the surrender of the King to the Scots and his execution by the Roundheads on 30th January 1649.

During this time the Lord Treasurer, in accordance with regular custom, had the custody of the Honours deposited in Edinburgh Castle, except during the sittings of Parliament, when they were delivered to the nobles who bore them in the procession, who then became their responsible guardians and took a receipt for them on delivering them back to the Captain of the Castle. Hitherto, Crown, Sceptre and Sword had regularly gone back to the Castle of Edinburgh on the termination of the sittings of Parliament, but the anxiety of those responsible for their safety was brought to a climax by Cromwell's victory at the battle of Dunbar on 3rd September 1650. Indeed, seven weeks later, Edinburgh Castle was taken by the English, but once more the Honours miraculously escaped. The Committee of Estates directed the Marquis of Argyll to 'secure' the Honours. He conveyed them to Perth, and on 17th September sent them to his kinman Sir Robert Campbell of Glenorchy, who kept them safely in his strong castle of Balloch by Loch Tay for the next two months. On 19th November Sir Robert returned them to Argyll, at the order of the Estates, to be brought back to Perth, and they duly appeared at the coronation of Charles II at Scone on 1st January 1651.

Charles the Second

The coronation of Charles II was the last at Scone and the last in Scotland. The ceremonies took place at a small kirk which had been built over the ruins of the ancient Abbey Church, burned in 1559. The procession was formed from the Palace, the Sword being carried by the Earl of Rothes, the Sceptre by the Earl of Crawfurd and Lindsay, and the Crown by the Marquess of Argyll immediately before the King. The church, we are told, had been duly prepared for the occasion, though the space was limited. Charles heard the sermon, signed the Covenant, and took the coronation oath. There was no anointing as at the coronation of Charles I and the Lord Chamberlain simply divested Charles of his princely robe and replaced it by the royal one. The Marquess of Argyll placed the Crown upon the King's head, whereon the Lyon King of Arms called the noblemen one by one to swear fealty to the King. The Lord Chancellor drew the Sword and handed it to Charles, who gave it to the Great Constable to be carried naked before him. The Earl of Crawfurd then placed the Sceptre in the royal hand and, after a proclamation of free pardons, the King showed himself to the people at the door of the church. Later there was a further swearing of fealty by the Lords, followed by a sermon of no ordinary length—'the exhortatioun was sumthing lairge.' The singing of the 20th Psalm and a blessing terminated the ceremony and the King returned in solemn procession to the Palace at Scone.

A romantic episode in the history of the Regalia

The Cromwellian forces continued to advance into the heart of Scotland, and perils were confronting the Covenanting party, so on 6th June 1651, the Earl Marischall was ordered by Parliament to remove the Honours to the stronghold of Dunnottar, a castle on the seaboard of Kincardineshire. Here they were defended by George Ogilvie of Barras, an officer to whom the command of the castle had been entrusted by the Earl Marischall, with a meagre garrison of 40 men, a lieutenant and two sergeants. But it soon became evident that the castle must eventually fall into the hands of the Cromwellian forces. The responsibility laid upon him as custodian of the Honours weighed heavily on the Governor, who could see no way out of the difficulty. At this crisis, a scheme for the removal of the royal emblems was devised by his wife, in consort with Christian Fletcher, wife of Mr James Granger, minister of the neighbouring parish of Kinneff. Mrs Granger's servant-girl came frequently to the cliffside near the castle 'on prentence of gathering dulse and tangles' until the besieging troops were well accustomed to her visits, and at length the opportunity occurred for her to carry away the Honours 'hid under dulse and coverings' and commit them to the care of Mrs Granger and her husband. The more romantic story of Mrs Granger herself conveying the Honours out of the Castle is now discredited.

They were lodged first, it is said, in the bottom of the bed at the manse until the minister had an opportunity for burying them safely in Kinneff Church. The account of their concealment is given by him in an acknowledgment to the Countess Marischall dated 31st March 1652.

'I, Mr James Granger, minister at Kinneff, grant me to have in my custody the Honours of the Kingdom, viz., the croun, sceptre, and sword. For the croun and sceptre I raised the pavement stone just before the pulpit, in the night tyme, and digged under it ane hole, and put them in there, and filled up the hole, and layed doun the stone just as it was before, and removed the mould that remained, that none would have discerned the stone to have been raised at all. The sword again, at the west end of the church, among some common saits that stand there, I digged down in the ground betwixt the twa foremost of these saits, and laid it doun within the case of it, and covered it up, as that removing the superfluous mould it could not be discerned by anybody; for if it shall please God to call me to my death before they be called for, your Ladyship will find them in that place.'

On 4th June 1652, Ogilvie was forced to surrender to the Cromwellian invaders, and one of the articles of capitulation provided 'That the Croun and Scepter of Scotland, together with all other ensigns of Regallitie, be delivered to mee, or a good account thereof, for the use of the Parliament.'

Bitter was the disappointment of the besiegers on finding the Regalia gone. The ex-Governor was mulcted in heavy fines on the ground of his having violated the terms of the capitulation, and he and his wife were rigorously imprisoned in the hope of extorting some information. But though Mrs Ogilvie gradually sank and died from the effects of her treatment, she adjured her husband in her last words never to reveal the secret entrusted to him.

For nine years the Regalia were kept in secrecy and safety until they were restored to King Charles II in 1660 at the instance of the Countess Marischall and returned to Edinburgh Castle. As rewards for preserving the Honours of the kingdom, the Hon. Sir John Keith, son of the Earl Marischall, was created Earl of Kintore and Knight Marischall with a yearly salary of £400, Ogilvie received the lesser honour of a baronetcy, while Mrs Granger, the heroine of this romantic episode, was awarded but two thousand merks 'as a testimony of their sense of her service.'

The Regalia of Scotland being thus fortunately preserved and restored to the public, continued to be produced as formerly during the sittings of the Scottish Parliament until the year 1707, when the Act of Union put an end to these time-honoured customs. When the Parliament of Scotland was finally dissolved, the Earl Marischall was called upon to surrender their custody to the Commissioners of the Treasury, but to guard against any attempt to remove them to England, the following clause was added to the 24th Article of the Treaty: 'And the Crown, Scepter and Sword of State, Records of Parliament and all other Records, Rolls and Registers whatsomever . . . continue to be keeped as they are in that part of the United Kingdome now called Scotland, and that they shall so remain in all tyme coming, notwithstanding of the Union.'

Thus the Honours of Scotland, on 26th March 1707, were locked up in the oak chest in the Crown Room and left to silence and seeming oblivion for more than a century. It is not surprising that after a while, when nothing was heard of them, and they had vanished from public sight, suspicions arose that the Treaty of Union had been quietly ignored, and the Regalia surreptitiously removed to England. A question, however, arose in 1794 regarding some missing records, and, on the chance of their having been deposited in the well-nigh forgotten chamber, the doors were opened under a Royal Warrant. The search was fruitless, but there stood the great oak chest known to have been the receptacle of the Regalia in 1707. As its key was lost, and the warrant gave the Commissioners no power to force the lock, it remained undisturbed, and once more the Crown Room was locked and secured.

At length, following the urgent efforts of Sir Walter Scott, the Prince Regent, afterwards George IV, issued a warrant dated 28th October 1817, to the Scottish Officers of State and to Sir Walter himself, to open the Crown Room and search for the Regalia. The Crown Room was accordingly opened in presence of the Commissioners on 4th February 1818. The Wizard of the North, with romantic enthusiasm, described the scene thus:

'The chest seemed to return a hollow and empty sound to the strokes of the hammer, and even those whose expectations had been most sanguine felt at the moment the probability of disappointment, and could not but be sensible that, should the result of the search confirm these forebodings, it would only serve to show that a national affront and injury had been sustained, for which it might be difficult, or rather impossible to obtain any redress. The joy was therefore extreme when, the ponderous lid of the chest being forced open, at the expense of some time and labour, the Regalia were discovered lying at the bottom covered with linen cloths, exactly as they had been left in the year

1707 ... The rejoicing was so general and sincere as plainly to show that, however altered in other respects, the people of Scotland had lost nothing of that national enthusiasm which formerly had displayed itself in grief for the loss of these emblematic Honours, and now was expressed in joy for their recovery.'

The Commissioners reported that the Regalia had in no way suffered from their long confinement in the chest apart from being 'tarnished and soiled with dust.'

So, after being secluded for over a hundred years, the Honours were restored to the people of Scotland on 4th February 1818 and, following on the report of the Commissioners, the original of which is preserved in the Register House, another Royal Warrant was issued on 8th July 1818, appointing the Keeper of the Great Seal of Scotland, the Keeper of the Privy Seal, His Majesty's Advocate, the Lord Clerk Register, and the Lord Justice Clerk Commissioners for the keeping of the Regalia. By virtue of its powers Sir Adam Ferguson, the friend and neighbour of Sir Walter Scott, was appointed Keeper, and the Honours of Scotland have been open to public inspection since that date, except during the period of the First and Second World Wars when they were removed to a place of concealment. In 1838 the separate office of Keeper was abolished and the custody of the Crown Room entrusted to the Queen's and Lord Treasurer's Remembrancer as the last survivor of the establishment of the ancient Scottish 'Commissioneris of the Thesaurarie'.

The Lord Treasurer's mace

When the Crown Room was searched in 1818, there was discovered in the oak chest, along with the Regalia, a silver-gilt rod or mace surmounted by a globe of rock crystal which was not mentioned in the Act of Delivery and Deposition of 1707. Sir Walter Scott states that this proved to be the mace of office peculiar to the Treasurer of Scotland, and that it had probably been deposited in the chest by the Earl of Glasgow. The Register of the Privy Council reveals that, in 1609, the Treasurer was ordered to carry a small walking rod and to have a silver mace carried before him, and there is further evidence that a Treasurer's mace existed in 1616, for it was, on the 17th December in that year, produced by Sir Gideon Murray of Elibank, Treasurer-Depute, before the Lords of the Privy Council, and by them delivered to the newly appointed Treasurer, the Earl of Mar.

Head of the Lord High Treasurer's mace

27

On the death of Sir Gideon Murray of Elibank in 1621, his son Sir Patrick Murray, on the orders of the Privy Council, handed over to the Earl of Mar, the Lord High Treasurer, the Honours, 'to witt, the crowne, swerd, and sceptour, togidder with his majesteis whole silver plaitt, quhairof his said umquhile fader had charge and keeping'. At an official inspection of the Honours by a Committee of the Privy Council on 7th July 1621, it was noted that the Sceptre 'wes in three peeceis, the heade quhairof hes beene brokin and mendit with wyre, and that the Swerd had the plumbett birsit and brokine . . . and the scabert thairof revin, birsit and brokine, wanting some peeceis oute of it.' On 10th July the Earl of Mar acknowledged before the Council the receipt of the Honours 'and of ane grite aik kist quhairin thay ar keepit, and of the silver plaitt, and maise callit the thesauraris maise, quhilk wes delyverit to him be the said umquhile Sir Gedeone in his awne tyme.'

The oak chest

The oak chest which contained the Regalia during their long seclusion from 1707–1818 is probably the same as that mentioned in 1621 and is worthy of a short description. It is made of Dantzig oak, appears to be of Scottish workmanship, and has been so constructed as to permit of its being taken into the Crown Room in pieces and afterwards put together, as the size of the door would not permit of its being carried in bodily. The chest is a characteristic specimen of those commonly used in Scotland during the sixteenth and seventeenth centuries, and it may be of interest to note the phrasing of the Act of Delivery and Depositation in 1707, that the Honours were lodged 'in an orderly manner in a chest within the said crown room.'

The sword belt of the Sword of State

The immunity from destruction which has so marvellously attended the Regalia of Scotland is one of the noteworthy features in their history; and the survival and preservation of the sword belt during internal dissensions, civil wars, and foreign invasions is indeed remarkable. As already mentioned, it accompanied the gift of the Sword of State by Pope Julius II to James IV in 1507.

Throughout the whole narrative of the siege of Dunnottar Castle by the Cromwellian forces no mention is made of the sword belt. The order for the delivery of the Regalia to Edinburgh Castle mentioned only the Crown, the Sceptre and the Sword of State, and it is probable that in these circumstances the belt was retained by Ogilvie, in the first place until a proper receipt for it was presented, and also as a piece of real evidence that he had had the Regalia in his possession. At any rate, the very existence of the belt was forgotten until, in 1790, it was discovered by Sir David Ogilvy, built into the garden wall of the ancestral House of Barras. On the death of Sir David Ogilvy it passed to his son and eventually to a descendant, the Rev. Samuel Ogilvy Baker, who graciously restored it to its proper place in the Scottish Regalia in 1892. So, more than two centuries after the siege of Dunnottar Castle, the sword belt was formally deposited in the Crown Room at the Castle on the 29th May 1893, by the Marquis of Breadalbane, Her Majesty's Lord High Commissioner.

The belt of the Sword of State consists of two distinct portions —the woven lace belt and the silver-gilt clasp or buckle. It is a magnificent specimen of woven lace work and has several

The oak chest which contained the Regalia from 1707 till 1818

interesting features. The arms of Pope Julius II are treated in exactly the same way in both the scabbard and the belt; and the ornament of oak-leaves and acorns, which formed part of his coat-of-arms, is of similar design in both. The length of the belt ranges, when buckled, from 28 inches to 59 inches. Fifty-nine inches is manifestly too large for an average waist, but might be suitable for hanging over the shoulder. Twenty-eight inches, on the other hand, is too small for an average shoulder belt; so, from the fact that two pairs of holes have been purposely made afterwards by less skilful hands, the inference may be drawn that it was for use on the slender figure of Queen Mary, or possibly for the infant coronation of King James V.

Belt of the Sword of State of Scotland

The ensigns of the Orders of the Garter and the Thistle

The other articles, consisting of the Collar and George of the Order of the Garter, the St Andrew of the Order of the Thistle, and a ruby and diamond ring were formerly kept in England and are assumed to have been in the possession of James VII when he fled to France in 1688. Long years afterwards, his grandson Henry, Cardinal of York, the last male descendant of the Stewarts, bequeathed them gratefully to George III who had considerately granted him a pension when ruined by the French Revolution. These are now shown along with the Regalia. They were deposited in the Crown Room in the presence of certain officers of State on the 18th December 1830, by order of William IV shortly after his accession to the throne.

The collar of the Order of the Garter

The collar consists of 21 garters, each $1\frac{1}{2}$ inches in diameter and having in the centre a double rose, enamelled in red and green. It measures just over 5 feet in length and is made throughout of gold.

The George of the Order of the Garter

The George is made of gold and enamelled in colours. It represents St George armed, sitting on horseback, encountering the dragon with a spear. The obverse is studded with 118 rose and table cut diamonds and the reverse is enamelled in various colours.

The St Andrew of the Order of the Thistle

The Jewel of St Andrew shows on one side the Patron Saint set round with twelve large rose diamonds and surmounted by a larger diamond, and on the other side a fine miniature, at one time thought to be of Princess Clementina Sobieski, wife of Prince James Francis Edward Stuart, but now believed to be that of Louise of Stolberg, Countess of Albany, the wife of Prince Charles Edward Stuart. The miniature is surrounded with a garter inlaid in blue enamel and covered by a hinged lid enamelled with a Scots thistle.

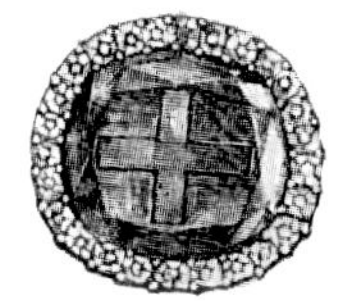

FRONT

BACK

The ruby and diamond finger ring (actual size)

The ruby ring

Tradition has described this ring as the Coronation Ring of Charles I, though there is no evidence to support this. It is made with a peculiar arrangement so that it might fit fingers of all sizes, being jointed like a bracelet with an exceptionally long spring to the snap and a number of notches in it, so that it may be enlarged or contracted at pleasure. The ring contains a large, pale-coloured ruby, engraved with a cross, and around it are set 26 small diamonds.

The ancient velvet cushion

In 1905, the ancient cushion (dating from about 1650), on which it is believed the Crown was formerly borne, was handed over for exhibition by Sir Patrick Keith Murray, Bt. Now kept in the National Museum of Antiquities, it is believed to have been retained at Dunnottar after the removal of the Honours and subsequently preserved at Ravelston and Ochtertyre.

The Great George (obverse and reverse); the St Andrew of the Order of the Thistle (showing the patron saint and a miniature of Louise of Stolberg, Countess of Albany); and the ruby and diamond ring with a section of the collar of the Order of the Garter